Peter Tully's

PICTURES of PAIG
Part III

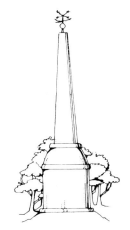

OBELISK PUBLICATIONS

Other Books in this Series

Peter Tully's Pictures of Paignton
Peter Tully's Pictures of Paignton Part II
Albert Labbett's Crediton Collection
Albert Labbett's Crediton Collection II
An Alphington Album, *P. Aplin & J. Gaskell*
The Dawlish Collection, *Bernard Chapman*
The Totnes Collection, *Bill Bennett*
Ian Jubb's Exeter Collection
Mike & Hilary Wreford's Okehampton Collection
Mike & Hilary Wreford's Okehampton Collection II
Mike & Hilary Wreford's Okehampton Collection III
Fred Tozer's Newton Abbot Album
Fred Tozer's Newton Abbot Album II
Pictorial Torquay, *Leslie Retallick*
Kingsteignton Collection, *Richard Harris*
A Chudleigh Collection
A Brixham Album
An Exeter Boyhood, *Frank Retter*
The Pubs and Inns of Ashburton, *Pete Webb*

For further details of these or any of our extensive
Devon titles, please contact us at 2 Church Hill,
Pinhoe, Exeter, EX4 9ER, Tel: (01392) 468556.

*Front cover: see page 25. Back cover pic: shows the Home and
Colonial Stores in Victoria Street. The manager, Mr Jim Pitman
(standing in the middle), lived for many years in Gerston Road
and was a prominent member of the local branch of the British
Legion. When the shop closed, probably in the mid-'50s, it was
then occupied by Millward Maxie (TV and Wireless) who moved
down from Palace Avenue.*

ISBN: 1 899073 13 2

2

Acknowledgements

As in Books I and II I freely acknowledge the great help I have
received from friends, known and unknown, who have enabled me
to collect yet a further selection of old photographs. I would
particularly like to thank the Devon Library Services, the Torbay
Borough Council Planning Dept, and Nicholas Horne of Totnes.
There must still be many old photos, lying around in cupboards and
boxes. I would be delighted to have a sight of them – who knows
– there may be a Book IV!

*This book is dedicated to my wife, Mary, whose patience
with my very untidy hobby has been wonderful.*

First Published in 1995 by Obelisk Publications
2 Church Hill, Pinhoe, Exeter, Devon
Designed by Chips and Sally Barber
Typeset by Sally Barber
Printed in Great Britain by
Maslands Ltd, Tiverton, Devon

Let's start off this third volume of old "Pictures of Paignton" with a real treat ... This wonderful photograph shows Mr Peter Pelosi and his ice cream cart outside Dellers Cafe in Torbay Road some time about 1913. He first arrived in Paignton with his mother in 1903 and soon set about establishing a chain of milk bars and ice cream parlours in Torbay.

Many folk will have fond memories of Pelosi's first ice cream parlour at 55 Torbay Road. This is how it looked in 1932. In 1938 it was modernised and fitted with an on-street serving window. However, with no discos, clubs or bowling alleys around at that time, it became a social mecca for visitors and locals alike. Following the success of this venture, Peter Pelosi's sons opened other shops. Ernest, the third oldest son, managed the Three Beaches outlet, Joe ran one at Brixham Quay and John managed the milk bar at Abbey Place in Torquay.

In 1953 Peter Pelosi celebrated his 50th anniversary of trading in Paignton in the best way possible, by inviting lots of local children along for free ice creams. The following year he died, his legacy being a lifetime of supplying the local populace, and a great many visitors, with ice creams from his kiosks at Paignton and Goodrington. Note the expressions of blissful anticipation!

Main Staircase. Dellers Café, Paignton.

Deller's Café.

Dellers has already had a passing mention but here are some views of the interior of a building that will hold fond memories for those Paigntonians old enough to recall halcyon days spent there.

At present, these premises at 32 Victoria Street are occupied by the Woolwich Building Society but, as the picture shows, others have been there before. This picture was taken in 1913. A few years later the ornate frontage was changed in appearance by the addition of black marble. In the interwar period Paignton was blessed with a number of main street jewellers – Goss Mabin in Torbay Road and Waltons in Hyde Road being but two of them. In 1971 Desmond Mortimer Ricks moved his business into Hyde Road, taking over the last private house, on the east side of that road, to be converted into a shop. Eventually Mr Ricks sold the business and the shop became a delicatessen, but today it stands empty.

Here we have four Winner Street shops as they looked in the 1920s/1930s. John Morrish's son became the first Prisoner of War to hail from Paignton. Many of the items displayed in the window are probably highly collectible these days. On the door is an advert for an imminent Paignton Carnival, which suggests that this picture was taken in the summer. The success of the event was vital for the hospital as in those pre-NHS days they were dependent on funds raised like this. The shop is today The Century of Playtime, a local museum of early toys and games. Gould's Stores were almost opposite the bottom of Clifton Road, next to the grassy plot at one time the home of the Labour Exchange before it moved into the large building on the left of the picture on Page 38. These premises, at 18 Winner Street, have been occupied for several years by the printing firm of Partington. Don't be fooled by the '60' on Carr and Quick's as today it's '127' and instead of wall to wall drinks, it's wall to wall carpets! In the first of this series of books I described the premises of the Co-op as their butchery department. In fact it was their Fruit, Fish and Poultry Department. Hopefully the picture opposite will put the record straight as **this** is their butchering department, about Christmas 1920. The Co-op's official newssheet, The Wheatsheaf, boasted that "Our Christmas show of prime meat…was highly appreciated, the general opinion being that it excelled any other dealers in town. Members can depend on their orders receiving prompt and careful attention."

9

Distins Court, in Winner Street, was named after a well-known Paignton family who, at one time, used to farm at Preston. Their buildings were traversed by Upper Manor Road. This 'Court', as it was known, was really only just a small cluster of buildings with access to them through this archway. In time the buildings decayed to such an extent that they were demolished before the Second World War. They were replaced, in part, by the extension to the Baptist church and also, in part, by a row of single-storey shops.

The message, "Salute the Soldier" seems well displayed in this 1942 photo. There was a national campaign to raise extra revenue to pay for the war effort. It was estimated, even then, that to fund the war it cost something in the region of eight million pounds per day! Here, then, was just one of the fund-raising activities for "Salute the Soldier Week". Butcher Freddie Matthews and various volunteers are seen here with his decorated horse and cart. Similar weeks were arranged for all the other armed forces. In the background is the public hall (Palace Avenue Theatre) that was known as the Garrison Theatre at that time. Mr and Mrs Matthews are on the left with Mrs Dorothy Butt beside them. The best seat, atop the cart, is taken by "John Bull" who is Julia Davis. Also featured are Thelma Butt and Freda Matthews.

The Palace Avenue Theatre is shown here without anyone around to obscure it this time. The building has played various roles in the life and entertainment of Paignton and has been accorded the nickname of "The Old Lady of Palace Avenue". It was designed by Messrs Couldrey, Bridgman and Lambhead. The last two named were upstanding Gentlemen who both served, for a time, as Chairmen of the Paignton Urban District Council. The original intention was to site the theatre where the central gardens now exist. Notice the canopy that covered the pavement and which afforded theatre-goers some protection during inclement weather. The age of progress is such that niceties like this don't exist today!

Another fine presentation by the Paignton Operatic, Dramatic and Choral Society! This time the production was The Student Prince performed in April 1957. Geoffrey Snelson was the producer, Margaret Warren was responsible for the choreography. John Hopwood was the musical director. On the left is Bill Coysh who was then Chairman of the operatic section. A special feature of these amateur productions was 'Civic Night' when members of the PUDC and various dignitaries from neighbouring towns were invited. The cast of The Student Prince included Jill Farrant, Bruce Lochtie, Howard Baker, Yvonne Wheaton, David Marshall, Cyril Eade, Bruce Seville, Vic Tomlin, Pamela Martin and Stan Bath.

(Opposite) This was Montpelier School's complex of buildings at Barcombe Hall. The school's roots went back to 1884 when it was founded at Montpelier, a house in Grosvenor Road, by the Rev J. M. Wheat. He was succeeded, in 1893, by Mr Bertram Bennett who served as Headmaster for thirty-three years until he was followed by F. L. Green. In 1927 the school moved to these more spacious surroundings at Barcombe Hall. "FL" retired in 1956. His daughter, Noelle, and his son-in-law, Richard Jordain, took over as Principals, whilst Martin Knapp was Headmaster. The assembled group, bottom right, are probably awaiting the arrival of a Naval helicopter on a recruiting drive. Alas the school fell on hard times and closed in 1985. The hall has been demolished and new houses and flats have since been built here.
And there's more … There were many small, independently run, private schools in Paignton in the first half of the twentieth century and pictured above is one that was called Monplaiser College. It was located in the corner house of Upper Polsham Road. Here the young lady students can be seen on the corner of the road, and also peering out of most of the windows of this large building.

Can you recognise where this temporary celebration arch was erected? The event was the Coronation of King George V and Queen Mary and took place in 1911. This Royal couple had a strong affection for Devon so it's appropriate that the local populace should go to even greater lengths to celebrate their coronation. Everyone in the picture is dressed in their Sunday-Best. If you haven't guessed, then this arch was built across a much narrower Conway Road at the St Michael's Road end of it.

"Long live Baden Powell" it says and it was so for this hero of Mafeking, during the South African War, lived to the ripe old age of 84. This photo was taken outside the New Pier Inn in Roundham Road, overlooking Paignton's harbour. Burch's Stores & Bakers in the background are now The Toby Jug. Flats now exist where the sheds are shown.

We move from a national hero to many local ones! Here we have some of the personnel from the 10th (Torbay) Battalion, Home Guard, taken some time around 1943/44. The Commanding Officer, Lt Col A. J. H. Slogget, DSO is featured here with some of his NCOs. Also in the picture, for those who may know them, is Bill Strike, Jim Pitman, Langley-Ellis, Knollys, Fursdon, Woosley and, of course, Rex the Labrador.

(Opposite) This is not the Home Guard in action! The occasion was the celebration of the Silver Jubilee of King George V and Queen Mary, 6 May 1935. A royal salute was fired by the 222nd Battery Royal Artillery at about 12.30 pm on Paignton Green. This particular Battery was the local Territorial unit based at the Drill Hall in York Road. The public was kept a safe distance from the volley of guns.

This photo, taken in the early 1870s, is of Fernham Villa, which was in Torquay Road next to the site of the old Palladium car park. It was taken by its owner at the time, Mr J. Macintyre. It shows his two daughters, Mina and Eliza, standing on the east-facing balcony. I believe he sold the property to Isaac Singer, of sewing machine fame, but it's difficult to confirm this as Singer bought so much property to lay out Oldway. In the 1930s it was owned by the local pathologist and General Practitioner, Dr Reynolds. He ran it as a private residence, nursing home and base for his practice. The inset picture shows a fire, which caused extensive damage in the early 1960s. The site is now Fernham Old People's Home.

And so it's a natural progression to consider one of Paignton's treasures – Oldway Mansion. Isaac Singer, a man of vision, built his 'Wigwam' by 1875, the year of his death, at the age of 64. When Paris Singer, his third son, inherited the property, he had grand ideas for it. The east and north elevations were bestowed with pillars to create a resemblance to the Palace of Versailles. The architect was the celebrated George Souden Bridgman. Don't be fooled by the scaffolding, which were wooden poles lashed together with rope. The alterations to the 'Wigwam' were carried out between 1904-07. To enhance the French atmosphere, he employed Monsieur Duchesne to lay out the grounds that so many people still enjoy so much.

Oldway has an eventful history and these three pictures simply serve to reflect some of the sadder times of this great house. Oldway was loaned by Paris Singer to be used as the American Women's War Hospital. The wounded of various nationalities, arriving at Paignton Station, were conveyed to Oldway by ambulance and charabanc. There were times when the trains bringing in these casualties stacked up so much that they reached back to Polsham Road. There were many different injuries and the staff had to possess a wide range of skills to cope with so many medical problems. It has been said that there were more funerals, in 1918, held in the hospital's chapel, built in the grounds, as a result of patients dying from influenza than from the wounds that brought them there in the first place. The hospital was laid out on a plan devised by Joan Bates, who was Paris singer's personal nurse. Later, as romance blossomed, Paris divorced his wife, Eugenie and married his nurse, Joan Bates, in Florida.

(Opposite) The Great Western Railway took over the lines of the South Devon Railway company in February 1876. Some years later they also opened a bus route between Paignton and Torquay. The drivers were the ones who wore the long coats because they were exposed to the elements, as can be seen from the open nature of the bus. This photo was taken in 1905 outside Paignton Station. It is doubtful

whether the ride would have been a very comfortable one with solid rubber tyres and hard, potentially bum-numbing wooden seats! The one consolation was that the journey was faster than the one on Mr Hyde Dendy's horse-drawn buses.

Paignton is Devon's best loved seaside resort with its distinctive red sands and sandstone headlands but it's one that has seen many changes over the years. The Esplanade looks very different in this photo but it is the hills in the background that have seen the greatest change. Gone are the fields of this view, to be replaced by miles of housing.

Staying in the same area but looking along the line of hotels, in 1897, along the front. A look at the photo is enough to show what a genteel age this must have been for there is no traffic and only of smattering of people strolling around. The Golden Jubilee Fountain can be seen on the right. The Park Hotel, as we know it, was six separate houses and The Fiesta was still Elbury Lodge. The ever-active Hyde Dendy had turned the next two privately owned properties, on the far right of the picture, into The Esplanade Hotel. This can be seen, in all its glory, on page 30 in the first edition of Pictures of Paignton.

This is the central portion of Paignton's sea front as it looked in the early 1950s. The wood and canvas windmill was erected on top of the main shelter and toilets. This was fronted by a sign, illuminated, by night, that said "Welcome to Paignton". Visitors loved to photograph the windmill at night but most ended up with a picture showing ten circles of light. The windmill was replaced in 1964 by a round conglomeration of lights, perhaps a forerunner of today's disco lighting. The old Summer Pavilion can be seen on the left with the rest gardens on the right, behind the trees.

But, by contrast, Paignton Green has not always been so peaceful, not even in the past! These three pictures show just how prized is this lovely, spacious and flat site. The view with the helter-skelter is of Hancock's Fair in about 1900. Each year at Paignton Regatta time they would arrive in town with their colourful rides and entertainments, much simpler delights than are the norm today. This they did until 1926 when a disastrous fire at Plymouth destroyed much of their equipment. Since then Anderton & Rowlands have filled the regatta slot. Initially the fair alternated its site between the central portion of the green and its north end. However the arrival of a bandstand and the complaints of the bandsmen at the noise generated by revellers at the fair prompted the fair always to be held on the North Green on the second Tuesday and Wednesday of August. In 1953 the PUDC granted an extra day, Monday, to help meet demand and keep everyone happy.

There are several beaches at Paignton and Goodrington has always been popular. The crowded beach scene is from the 1960s, a time when the beach huts on Goodrington South Sands were a mix of council and privately owned ones. Hopkins ran the tea hut, Addisons ran the more up-market cafe, Pelosis had the ice cream kiosk and, I believe, Harveys had the shellfish stall. The trampolines proved to be successful but that was before Quay West and its water flumes! A miniature steam train began running in 1955 where the driver straddled the tender. This diesel made its first appearance in 1964 and ran from beside Hopkin's Tea Hut up to the far end of the sands near the Retreat.

This is what Goodrington looked like about a century ago, how things have changed right across the whole scene. The farmhouse in the foreground was owned by the Misses Brown and demolished in 1934 as part of the council's provision of seaside amenities. Paradise Walk has yet to be constructed on the right. As can be seen there were no houses at Three Beaches, Waterside, or along Goodrington Road up to White Rock and nothing at Cherry Brook. The building on the right of the photo is 'Simla', long since demolished and the hill has been excavated and used to fill in what is now Quay West's car park.

This is The Retreat when it was nothing more than a grassy area without the protection of any limestone wall. The children only had a few swings on which to play in this forerunner of what was to become Peter Pan's Playground in the 1930s. This picture provides a better view of 'Simla', the house with an Indian name, on the hill.

Little more can be said of this view of The Retreat at the south end of Goodrington South Sands other than that it shows the type of tents let out by the Council. In "Pictures of Paignton Part II" (page 7) there is a similar view included but taken looking the other way towards Roundham Head. Here we look towards Waterside. The headland in the murky distance to the left is the great limestone promontory of Berry Head.

Well, here is Waterside Camp in all its glory as it looked in 1953, the year in which mains drainage was introduced. It was a time when cars and camping were beginning to catch on after the austerity of the war. A camp shop, some toilets, a tent or a small caravan, if your means ran to it, and that was it! Waterside Camp was owned by a group of businessmen until the 1930s. The camp was then managed by Mr & Mrs Corney who lived in the detached house by the entrance. Here they had a kiosk, which supplied the campers' needs. Later in that same decade it was sold to the Paignton Urban District Council for £17,000.

Although this picture is a Sunday School treat the expressions on the faces of these youngsters do not indicate that a great time is being had by all. Until 1896 men and women were not allowed to bathe in the sea together! Women were afforded the privilege of using Paignton Beach whilst the men had to use the beach at Preston. Modesty was the order of the day and these bathing machines of Mr Hyde Dendy saw to it that decency prevailed. In the 1960s I owned the last surviving bathing machine from Paignton and kept it in my garden in Adelphi Road, which, incidentally, was formerly Mr Couldrey's kitchen garden. When I sold the house I had to pay Jimmy Thorpe to come, break it up and remove it. This was before I discovered "Old Paignton". I guess losing a treasure like this must happen to a lot of people. If only I'd known then …

34

Above is Preston House as it looked in the late 1940s. From 1910 it was the home of the Butland family who previously had lived at Occombe House. The family have lived in Paignton for nearly four hundred years and were the third name in the parish registers. They were prominent landowners in this part of the town along with the Distens who owned Manor House. The Butland estates extended from Hollacombe back out to Five Lanes. It was the custom for the eldest son to bear the name Robert. This practice was continued until the last Robert Butland, a bachelor, died in the early 1950s. This property was then sold to the PUDC who demolished it, turning it into the car park that now adjoins the Preston Conservative Club. Fortunately they retained the grounds which are now a public park. At one time a continuous red sandstone wall ran from 365 Torquay Road to the club, with but one small door giving access. This was located opposite Paris Road. The main entrance to Preston House was in Old Torquay Road but is now walled up. The only trace is a kink in the wall where the large wooden gate once hung.

Opposite is a view that we have featured, from different angles in both "Pictures of Paignton" (Page 27) and "Pictures of Paignton II" (Page 48). This one was taken in 1947 and shows the wartime anti-camouflage paint on the major rectangular buildings and the rocket site just below the signal box, which itself has long since disappeared. Gas produced here was used to inflate barrage balloons protecting our towns, cities and military installations. The gas holders have gone and now this is a pleasant public park. The two areas of allotments have fallen into disuse but the Mencap Centre has been built on the Bay View Terrace allotments. The fir trees, lower right, have matured. The small building on the opposite side of the road to the gas holders was, at one time, the gas company's showrooms. It then became their recreational club before finally being demolished.

It's amazing how places change before our very eyes, places that we have known all our lives and then they are, as Monty Python may have said, now "Something completely different". These pictures were all taken in the 1970s, two of them in 1979. The photo above shows what is now the exit for the Gerston relief road, now Great Western Road. It shows Jack Waters' old house on the left, which was demolished in the late 1980s. It also shows the premises of the old Torbay Mill, occupied, in this photo, by the Torbay Tyre Service. Behind them were W. H. Williams & Son, wholesale newagents. All these premises, which abutted onto Station Lane, have gone now. The top right picture shows the former Paignton Station Goods Yard that closed to commercial traffic on 4 December 1967, all goods subsequently being delivered from Newton Abbot. The warehouses in the background were once owned by Holman's Corn and Forage Merchants. Later they were occupied by a firm of shop fitters. The picture bottom right is taken from the Sands Road level crossing. On the left is Sands Road garage, at one time owned by Mr Murrin. Behind this was the Electric Light Company's premises, close to the already mentioned Holman's. But all these lights have been dimmed now and there's not even a whiff of Mike Cornish's crab-pot business, that was also here, wafting on the wind!

There has been a garage at the junction of Totnes Road and Winner Street for many years. These two early snapshots were probably taken in the 1920s. Two of them show West End Garage but at different times, one before the advent of petrol pumps and the other shortly after their introduction. On the pre-pump photograph there is an advert for Pratt's Perfection Spirit, a vital fluid that came in 5 gallon drums and had to be distributed by hand pumps. This was probably the forerunner of some very famous petrols – Shell, British Petroleum (B P). The post-petrol pump picture, for those who like teasing tongue twisters, shows pumps that had a small hand operated dial that you set at the number of gallons required. A large handle was turned, which pumped the petrol into a large glass bowl, a gallon at a time. Reversing the handle, when the glass was full, allowed the petrol to drain into the car's tank. Filling up could be a long and arduous task, if you had the good fortune to be one of the few car owners of the day. The site, at this road junction, is still a garage –Torbay Motors – and is owned by the Snowden family. The third picture, of a typical car of the time, is of John Sutton and his mother on Paignton sea front, also in the late 1920s.

And there were lorries around as well that looked just like these. They are festooned in bunting and flags so it's likely that they have been decorated to be a trade entry in Paignton Carnival. Although this brewery had their HQ in Taunton, their presence in Paignton was there for all to see from their pubs to their extensive premises which were in Church Street, opposite the parish church and extended all the way to Princes Street. Their trade mark was a black horse and their ales and stouts were popular with both tied and free houses. The brewery, its stores and yard, was closed in the 1980s and the site is now occupied by St John's Court, a very grand block of sheltered flats.

Although I wouldn't wish to be so precise, my wife insists that this photograph was taken in 1929! One thing is certain and that is the GFS on the banner stands for the Girls' Friendly Society and they look friendly enough, don't they? This picture, taken at the parish church, provides a good opportunity to study the fashion and hair styles of that era. Unfortunately, prior to publication, nobody has managed to identify any of the ladies. No doubt many of the descendants and relations will come forward now that it's too late! I think this picture was taken in the church hall that adjoined the parish church at this time but which is now absorbed into the Paignton Hospital. It appears in the photo on the opposite page! The new church hall is, of course, in the vicarage garden near the Coverdale Tower.

Here we have a few pictures from nearby Littlegate Road. The one below, taken in the 1980s, shows the premises of Blackler's, at one time occupied by Webber and Steadham. The two garages on the right were formerly used by the Ambulance service. The picture on the right is of the Old Mill, now demolished and nothing more than a memory. It was a building of considerable size that stood to the left of the church tower in the view shown below. The water for this mill came from the overflow that was taken from Waterleat to the Bishop's Palace. It flowed along the leat in Winner St into this area of Littlegate Road and became known as The Mill Pool.

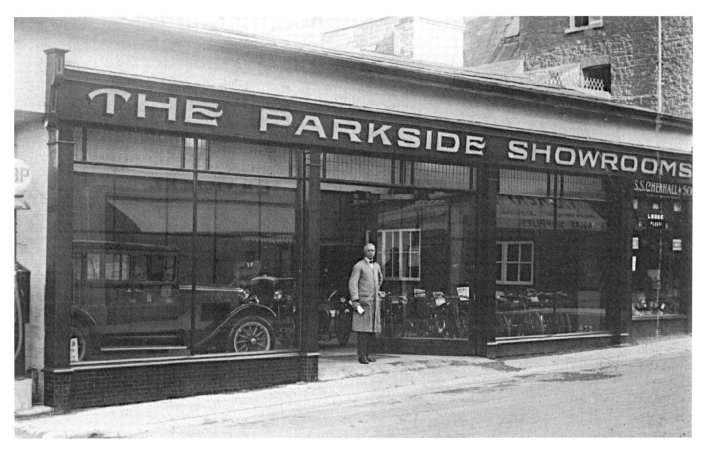

Parkside is the narrow side street, opposite the Torbay Cinema, that goes down to the Victoria Shopping Centre. The Parkside Showrooms are where you went, in the 1920s, if you wanted the latest model of car or motorcycle and some fine vehicles can be glimpsed in the showroom window. The firm of Chenhall's continues to trade in motor cars but not at this location, having moved out onto the Totnes Road near the Parkers Arms in Collaton St Mary where they specialise in BMWs. This picture was taken on 24 May 1927. The premises now house a fish and chip business.

The pictures on these two pages begin to show what lengths our forefathers went to in order to keep this South Devon seaside resort well watered. This labelled picture postcard view shows the dam and works under construction at Venford on Dartmoor. The dam site was on the edge of Holne Moor, some 15 miles WNW of Paignton, as the crow flies. In 1901 a tendered figure of £27,853 was accepted as a price to build the dam and work was commenced. However, faulty strata in the dam's foundations added extra costs and the final sum charged by the constructors, Hawkins & Best of Teignmouth, was £119,697.13s.6d. However, Paignton had grown so quickly in the eight years whilst construction took place that the trunk main was not big enough to convey sufficient water in summertime when the visitors came in large numbers. A second trunk main was added in 1909.

On 29 December 1905 the first water from Venford reached Paignton for testing purposes. The road over the dam, shown in this picture, was completed in May 1907. The following month the works were officially opened by the Member of Parliament, Mr F. Layland-Barratt. This photo also shows the charabanc and the horse-drawn vehicle used to carry the dignitaries to the ceremony. The water, from here, was regarded as a wonderful supply of soft pure water. Paignton kept its own supply until the water industry was nationalised after the Second World War and then it was obliged to share its treasured elixir with other places.

Opposite, at the bottom, we have some angelic mortals from the Paignton Parish Church. They were all assembled for the inauguration of the Guild of St Stephen for servers. The vicar at that time, in the early 1960s, was Preb. Molland. The picture at the top left of the opposite page had a caption that we cropped off for it includes an awful spelling mistake. It informed us that this was a stone laying ceremony at St John's Vicarage in 1910. The third picture on the page shows the bell ringers of the parish church in the 1940s. The name of the youngest one is not known but the others from left to right are: Tom Connings, Charlie Austin, Bill Allwood, Alf Pope and George Langworthy. Above is a picture that dates back to 1956 when The Church of England's Men's Society stepped into the vicarage garden. Although it's possible to name most of them the mists of time have clouded a few from our memory so I apologise for the gaps.

Back Row (L to R): Doug Tucker, Sgt. Allway, ? Baker, Jim Dinham, Ted Davies, Harold Nicholson, Sidney Wigglesworth, Norman Elliott, John Hopwood, Joe Finch, Len Smith, Bob Jones, Mr Higgs, Mr Bagg, Mr Balment?, Arthur Day, Harry Stratton and Godfrey Farrant. Middle Row: Lew Wingfield, Mr Wills, ?, ?, Ted Browne, Ivor Williams, ?, Cliff Pritchard, Mr Pengelly, Mr Shilston, Mr Rundle, Ted Webber. Front Row: Bill Coysh, Father Chevalier, Father Rundle,?, ?, Ray Valentine, Rev Chic Pedley, Seymour Bone, Father Callard, Mr Simpkins, Mr Reilley.

There are quite a few smiling faces in this photo taken at The Chairman's Ball of Paignton Urban District Council in 1954-55, probably held in Paignton's Palace Hotel. The chairman, in office that year, was Mr Alf Steart, complete with badge of office, of the Old Manor Inn. His term in office followed that of Jimmy Tremeer. He, in turn, was succeeded by Maurice Bishop. This long line of distinguished chairmen stretched back to the turn of the century when Robert Waycott held the position. Also in the photo, Back row, from L to R: Harry Cove-Clark, (?), Fred Tully (my father), Jack Wills, Frank May, George Cornelius, Jim Mason, Mrs Cove-Clark. Front row: Mrs Tully (my mother), Mrs Wills, Mrs and Mr Steart, Mrs Cornelius, Mrs May and Valerie May.

This has been a difficult photo to identify but I believe that it is of the Paignton Male Voice Choir, or possibly a breakaway group, the Kingsley Male Voice Choir, in about 1946. This I haven't been able to confirm. The choir had won a challenge shield and are shown here in Queen's Park with their proud conductor, Percy Pearce. A large number of well-known Paigntonians are featured and, as before, I apologise for not being able to identify everyone who was present on that occasion all those years ago. Still it should still stir a few memories! Back row, L to R: Les Wotton, George "Jock" Harris, ?, ?, Joe Cartledge?, Harold Reed, ?, ?, Middle row: Bill Stewart, Bill Edworthy, Edward Collins, Bill Dymond, Syd Rowell, Sid Beer, Percy Robins, Ron Lake, George Bradford, Stan Bath, and Sam Underhay. Front row: Les Burt, Jimmy Lidgey, Harold Hedges, Cyril Foster, Percy Pearce, Eileen Byrne (Accompanist), Len Thomas, Wilf Haywood, Roy Atkinson and George Widdicombe.

We finish this third collection of "Pictures of Paignton" with this early view, probably about 1880, of Paignton's sea front. The imposing terrace on the left is Adelphi Terrace, which was mainly constructed with stone salvaged from the demolition of Torbay House. The terrace was originally built as a row of separate residences –The Esplanade Hotel, formerly The Hydro, started life as a private house then became a nursing home in the early 1900s. It became a hotel in the 1920s. I think that the last one to be a private house belonged to Mr T. Mitchell-Fox who occupied the last house next to Adelphi Road. After the Second World War this became the premises of the Ministry of Pensions and after that the Ministry of Works.

The Green, as it appears in this picture, came about as the result of the generosity of two men, although there was method in their giving land to the town. Both were speculators in property and intended to build villas along the lower Esplanade Road. At the time the space was no more than a tract of sand dunes. By giving Polsham Green, now known as the North Green, to the council Mr MacLean ensured that a sea wall would be built at no cost to himself and the safety that afforded made his villas a much better proposition to any would-be purchaser, the sea having made many incursions in earlier years. The wall was built, in 1868, at a cost of £1,272.10s.0d. The owner of Torbay House, Mr Fletcher died and his trustees made over the southern half of the dunes to complete the space now shown in this view. The upper Esplanade was officially closed to vehicles, for the first time, from May to September in 1926. However cars were permitted to park on The Green until 1934 for the fee of 1/6d per day (about seven pence). By this time the number of cars visiting the resort had swollen to such a level that an alternative car park was established at Victoria Park and parking on The Green was banned.